Life Processes

ADAPTATION

Steve Parker

H www.heinemann.co.uk/library
Visit our website to find out more information about Heinemann Library books.

To order:
☎ Phone 44 (0) 1865 888112
🖹 Send a fax to 44 (0) 1865 31 4091
🖥 Visit the Heinemann Bookshop at www.heinemann.co.uk/library to browse our catalogue and order online.

First published in Great Britain by Heinemann Library, Halley Court, Jordan Hill, Oxford OX2 8EJ, part of Harcourt Education.
Heinemann is a registered trademark of Harcourt Education Ltd.

Editorial: Clare Lewis
Design: David Poole and Kamae Design
Picture Research: Melissa Allison
Production: Helen McCreath

Printed and bound in China by WKT

10 digit ISBN 0 431 17448 2
13 digit ISBN 978 0 431 17448 8

10 09 08 07 06

10 9 8 7 6 5 4 3 2 1

British Library Cataloguing in Publication Data

Parker, Steve
Life Processes: Adaptation – 2nd edition
578.4
A full catalogue record for this book is available from the British Library.

Acknowledgements

The publishers would like to thank the following for permission to reproduce photographs:
Bruce Coleman Collection: Mary Plage p.**14**; Corbis: Daniel Samuel Robbins p.**9**; NHPA: p.**20**, NA Callow p.**4**, David Middleton p.**4**, A.N.T. p.**7**, p.**24**, Darek Karp p.**8**, Stephen Dalton pp.**10**, **16**, **28**, Anthony Bannister pp.**11**, **25**, Martin Harvey pp.**12**, **15**, Dr Eckart Pott p.**13**, Hellio & Van Ingen p.**17**, GJ Cambridge p.**18**, EA Janes p.**19**, Roy Waller p.**19**, Norbert Wu p.**21**, B & C Alexander p.**22**, John Shaw p.**23**, Daniel Heuclin p.**25**, David Hosking p.**27**, Vincente Gardia Canseco p.**29**; Oxford Scientific Films: Daniel J Cox p.**4**, Colin Milkins p.**6**, Michael Fogden p.**10**, Richard Herrmann p.**20**, Roland Mayr p.**26**, Sean Morris p.**27**.

Cover photograph of a Demidoff bushbaby, reproduced with permission of NaturePL.com/ Bruce Davidson.

The publishers would like to thank Mary Jones for her assistance in the preparation of this book.

Every effort has been made to contact copyright holders of any material reproduced in this book. Any omissions will be rectified in subsequent printings if notice is given to the publishers.

The paper used to print this book comes from sustainable resources.

CONTENTS

Any words appearing in the text in bold, **like this**, are explained in the glossary.

A VARIETY OF HABITATS

The world has many different types of **habitat**, such as mountains, lakes, woods, and seashores. Most animals, plants, and other living things are **adapted** to one particular habitat. This is so common and natural that we rarely notice it. However, if we picture a living thing in the wrong habitat, the idea of adaptation becomes more obvious.

Suppose that a dolphin and a camel suddenly swapped places. The dolphin would not last long in a baking desert, with no water and too much heat. A camel could not survive in the open sea. It can hardly swim and would soon drown. Neither type of animal is adapted to the other's habitat.

▲ The dolphin's smooth, streamlined body slips at speed through the sea.

► Small creatures such as shieldbugs are coloured to blend into their surroundings so that they are noticed less by **predators**.

NEEDS FOR SURVIVAL

Living things have certain needs or requirements from their habitat, if they are to survive. These include:

- Energy to power their bodily life processes. Plants obtain their energy from sunlight and animals get theirs from food.
- Raw materials and **nutrients** for growth, body maintenance, and repair. Animals get these from food and plants from air and soil.
- Oxygen, the invisible gas in the air around us. Almost all living things need oxygen to survive.
- Water – life cannot exist without it.
- Shelter and protection from bad conditions such as harsh weather, and also from predators.
- A mate for breeding. This is not vital for an individual to stay alive, but it is essential if its **species** is to continue.

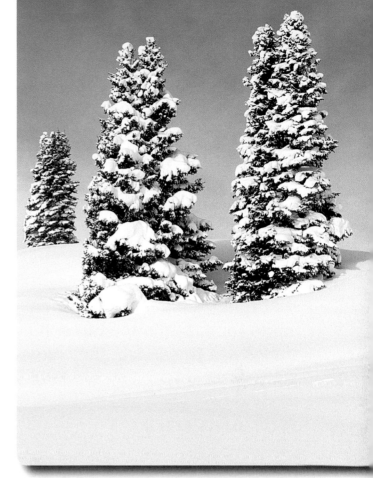

▲ Coniferous tree branches can flex and slope down so that snow slips off, without piling up and breaking the branch.

In each habitat living things face problems in obtaining these needs. This book shows how they have adapted to solve the problems and survive in the many different habitats on Earth.

ON THE MOVE

One example of an adaptation is a body feature that enables an animal to move effectively in its habitat. For example:

- A fish has a broad tail and fins to push itself through the water.
- A bird has flapping wings to carry it through the air.
- A mole has broad, strong front paws to dig through soil.
- A gazelle has long legs to run at speed across the grasslands.
- A monkey has long, flexible limbs with grasping hands and feet, to swing through the forest branches.

CHANGING CONDITIONS

Conditions in a habitat are always changing. Each day the Sun rises bringing light and warmth. The weather brings changes such as winds, storms, frost, and snow. On the seashore the tides rise and fall. These are all changes in the non-living world. Changes also happen in the living world. Sometimes animals such as locusts, lemmings, or rabbits breed in vast numbers. They eat so much that other animals, who normally eat the same food, begin to starve. If living things are to survive, they must cope with all these varying conditions.

HOT AND COLD

One of the main changes every day is the rise and fall in temperature, which happens as the Sun rises and sets. Most animals are **cold-blooded** and their activity is greatly affected by the surrounding temperature. After a cool night, a snake crawls slowly into the morning Sun and basks in its rays. Soon the snake is warm enough to move fast and pursue prey. As dusk falls and the temperature drops, the snake cools down again and can only move slowly. So it hides under a sheltering rock for the night.

► The barnacle's life is ruled by the twice daily rise and fall of the tides.

SIMILAR ANIMALS, DIFFERENT ADAPTATIONS

There are many examples of similar creatures, from the same animal group, that are adapted to different habitats.

- The African hare and American jackrabbit have very long legs and ears, and short fur. These features help the hare's body to lose warmth in the very hot conditions of its desert home.
- The Arctic hare has shorter legs and ears, and very long, thick fur. These features help to prevent loss of body warmth in the very cold habitat of the far north.

ADAPTED TO THE DARK

Each day also brings changes in light levels, which affect many living things. Some animals are **nocturnal**, which means they are active at night. They include moths, mice, owls, and bats. They are adapted to finding their way in the dark by various means, for example, the owl has extra-large eyes and the bat makes high-pitched squeaking sounds that bounce off nearby objects.

◄ Mice have huge eyes and long whiskers as adaptations to being nocturnal.

TYPES OF ADAPTATIONS

- Overall shape: A worm is long and thin to burrow through soil. A leaf is broad and flat to catch sunlight.
- Colour and pattern: The green tree frog is coloured to sit unnoticed among green leaves.
- Body parts: A part of the body may be adapted for a certain task, for example, the long fangs of a viper which stab venom (poison) into its prey.
- Internal workings: The chemical life processes of a living thing may show adaptations. The presence of a natural chemical **anti-freeze** in the bodies of ice-worms allows them to live in the freezing temperatures inside glaciers.

SIMILAR ADAPTATIONS, DIFFERENT ANIMALS

There are many examples of varied creatures, from different animal groups, that have similar adaptations because they live in the same habitat.

- Frogs, lizards, and squirrels that live in trees have long, slim, grasping fingers to hold on to the branches.
- Frogs, lizards, and squirrels that live on the ground have shorter, stubbier fingers for walking and running on hard surfaces.

LIFE IN THE MOUNTAINS

Compared to the surrounding lowlands, mountains are generally cold, wet, and windy. Very high mountains have snow and ice on the upper slopes. Also the air becomes thinner or less dense with height, so there is less of the vital gas oxygen that living things need to breathe. So the higher a mountain, the more severe the conditions for life. Mountain animals and plants are adapted in many ways to withstand these tough conditions.

LOWER PLANT ZONES

On many mountains, plants grow at certain levels or zones. There are broadleaved woodlands at the base. The foothills are cloaked with conifer trees that have thin, tough, needle-like leaves to survive long, cold winters. Increasing cold, snow, and wind mean that tall trees cannot survive above a certain height, called the tree line. So the next highest zone may be bushy scrub with hardy plants such as heathers. These have tough leaves and woody stems that are not easily damaged by strong winds.

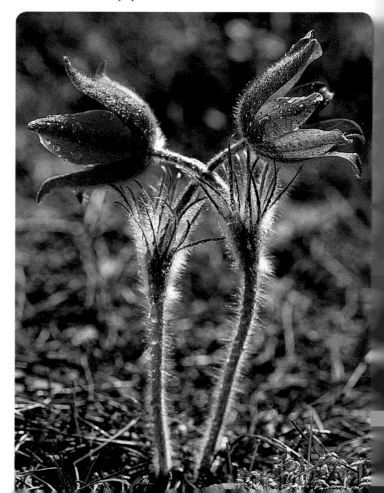

DID YOU KNOW ?

- Yaks have the longest fur of any mammal, growing up to one metre in length.
- Plants such as edelweiss have fine hairs on their leaves to keep out cold and keep in moisture.

► The alpine pasque flower, like the edelweiss, is adapted to harsh mountain conditions.

UP AND DOWN

Many larger mountain animals, such as chamois in Europe and yak in Asia, make yearly journeys called **migrations**. They walk up to the higher slopes in spring to be ready for the summer when the alpine meadow plants grow quickly. In autumn they return to the lower slopes and the shelter of the forests. Predators such as wolves and snow leopards follow them on the journey.

▲ Yaks are adapted to living high up in the Himalaya mountains.

HIGHER PLANT ZONES

Above the scrub zone are short grasses and herbs – the alpine meadow. These grasses are low-growing in cushion or rosette shapes, to avoid the fierce winds. Many alpine plants such as giant groundsel have developed adaptations such as hairy leaves to keep out the frost and keep in moisture, since the soil is thin and rain soon races away down the steep slopes. Higher still among the icy rocks and crags, no types of plant can survive.

MOUNTAIN ANIMALS

Small creatures such as insects and spiders can survive in the high mountains by feeding on bits of dead plants and animals, blown up the slopes by strong winds. Birds such as condors soar over the peaks watching for dead or dying victims. Mountain mammals such as chinchillas and vicunas in South America, and yak in Asia, have very long, thick fur to keep in body warmth. Like the mountain goat, chamois, and Siberian ibex, they have strong legs and feet to grip the rocks and ice as they move at speed across the steep slopes.

IN THE FOREST

Regions with a moist tropical climate have ideal conditions for plant life. There is year-round warmth and light, plenty of water, and minerals and nutrients in the soil. The thriving variety of plants in turn supports a vast range of animals, making tropical forests the richest habitats on Earth for wildlife. However, there are other kinds of forests where conditions are less favourable. Living things here have very different adaptations.

PLENTIFUL LIFE

The tropical rainforest habitat is perfect for life in all shapes, forms, and colours. Plants and animals do not have to battle for survival against the physical conditions. However, so many life-forms packed so close together means an abundance of predators, **parasites**, competitors for food, shelter and living space, and rivals for breeding. Living things must battle with each other rather than with the physical conditions.

▲ The macaw's bright colours and loud squawking warn other birds that this patch of tropical forest is occupied.

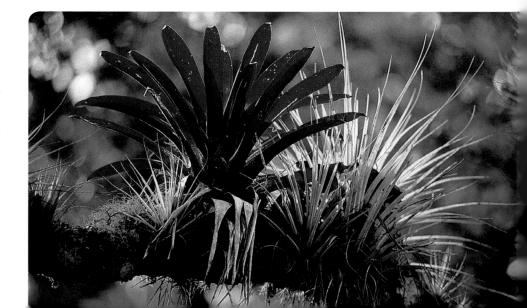

► The ground in a tropical forest is dark, so **epiphytic** plants like these bromeliads grow high up among the branches nearer the light.

COPING WITH COLD

In **temperate** regions, winter is shutdown time. Broad-leaved trees lose their leaves. Insects die off and leave tough-cased eggs to survive the cold. Dormice, marmots, and similar creatures **hibernate** (go into a deep winter sleep). Squirrels rest in their nests, coming out occasionally to dig up nuts and other food that they buried in autumn. Some small birds such as swifts and warblers migrate, flying long distances to warmer regions. All of these are adaptations to survive the cold of winter.

FROZEN SOLID

In the far north and south, winters are even longer and colder. Conifer trees such as pines, firs, and spruces are adapted to these severe climates. Their leaves are small, tough, and resist frost and icy winds. Their sloping branches allow snow to slip off before it becomes too heavy and breaks the branch.

Animals also have many ways of surviving these long winters. Frogs such as the spring peeper, the Siberian salamander, and reptiles such as painted turtles, can all withstand being frozen almost solid. Their bodies have high levels of anti-freeze substances so they can thaw back to life in the spring.

HOW TO HIDE IN THE FOREST

Many animals show amazing adaptations for **camouflage** by resembling parts of trees and bushes. They blend into the forest surroundings and are less obvious to predators.

- Stick insects look like twigs.
- Leaf insects resemble green forest leaves.
- Thornbugs and scalebugs are shaped like tree thorns.
- Moths or butterflies resting on tree trunks look like bark or old leaves.
- Spiders and mantises have bright colours to blend in with flowers.

► Looper caterpillars "freeze" to look like bugs or small twigs. A spider has not recognized this caterpillar.

ROLLING GRASSLANDS

Where the climate is too dry for trees, but too moist for a desert, grasses grow. They cover the land as far as the eye can see. The grassland habitat supports a huge quantity of life. However, animals have few trees or bushes to provide shade and shelter, and many struggle to survive the long, dry season. There is also the ever-present risk of a bushfire or a sudden flood when the rains come.

▼ Large plains mammals, such as giraffes in Africa, have long legs to race away from predators.

THE PRAIRIES

On the **prairies** (grasslands) of North America, the largest animals are bison. Being grazers they have wide, flat teeth for munching grass all day. Their huge size, and living together in herds, are adaptations for self-defence against predators such as wolves. Like many large grazers, bison migrate from a dry region to find better grazing elsewhere. However, this is no longer such a common sight. Bison numbers were hugely reduced by human hunters and the prairies are now used for farming. On African grasslands, called savannah, zebra and wildebeest have similar herd-dwelling lives.

BIG BIRDS

Grasslands and open scrub are home to the world's largest birds. These are ostriches in Africa, emus in Australia, and rheas on the pampas (grasslands) of South America. None of these birds can fly. They all have long, powerful legs to run away from predators, and sharp toe claws to kick out in defence.

LIVING LOW DOWN

Smaller grassland animals have less defence against predators so many dig tunnels and burrows. In North America prairie dogs form huge underground townships. As they feed on the surface a few prairie dogs are always watching for danger. They yip and bark if a hawk, fox, or similar predator comes near. African naked mole rats stay in their tunnel networks all of their lives. These strange mammals live in a **colony** like bees or ants. Only one female, the queen, breeds. The others are workers who dig tunnels and gather plant roots and other food.

▼ Dung beetles collect and bury dung from grassland mammals as food for their developing grubs.

CITY IN THE COUNTRYSIDE

Termites are small, pale, thin-skinned insects that would soon die in hot sun so they adapt small patches of grassland for their own needs. They build a tall mound from mud and dig a huge nest underneath. Here a million or more termites live in a cool, moist, underground city. Snakes, foxes, and even cheetahs use the hardened mounds for shelter, and owls and other birds perch on them.

DID YOU KNOW ?

Some animals and plants, such as acacia trees and ants, have special relationships. The ants bite and sting animals that try to eat the tree's leaves. In return, the thorny acacia provides the ants with a protected place to live. This type of relationship, where both partners benefit, is called **symbiosis**.

FLOWING WATERS

A typical river is not one habitat but many. In the hills, its gathering waters rush fast and foaming over a stony bed. When the river reaches lower plains it flows in wide loops, or **meanders**, and its current decreases so that sand and silt collect along its banks. As it enters the sea at its mouth or **estuary**, it slows still further and its fresh water mixes with salty seawater. Different animals and plants are adapted to these different parts of the river.

THE YOUNG RIVER

Near the river's start the fast current sweeps away small plants, animals, and bits of food. However, a few animals are suited to these conditions. Stonefly **larvae** (young) have low, flattened bodies and strong, wide-set, clawed legs to grip the pebbles on the bottom. Fish called bullheads also have low, flat bodies and hide among the stones too, where the river flow is slower.

▲ Dippers are land birds, but have adapted to diving for food in fast flowing upland streams.

THE MATURE RIVER

As the river's waters slow, nutrient-rich mud collects on the bottom and bank. Plants such as reeds and rushes take root, providing food and shelter for animals and fish. Larger predatory fish such as perch and pike thrive here, eating the plentiful smaller prey of worms, water insects, and young fish. Catfish and crayfish come out from their holes at night to **scavenge**.

THE ESTUARY

Near the sea, the fresh river water mixes with the sea's salty water. Salty water can cause great problems for freshwater animals because it affects their body chemistry. Certain fish, such as mullet, are adapted to this in-between watery world as are shellfish like winkles, oysters, and mussels.

MANGROVE SWAMPS

Along some sheltered tropical coasts, mangroves form huge swamps. The thick seashore mud contains little oxygen but mangrove trees have roots that stick up into the air and water, to take in extra oxygen. Mudskippers are also adapted to this habitat. These small fish hold pools of water in their large **gill** chambers, so they can survive in air for many minutes. Their front fins are like muscular arms and they use them to skitter across the mudflats.

ALTERING THE HABITAT

Beavers, like other rodents such as rats and squirrels, have large front teeth for gnawing. They gnaw down branches and small trees and drag these into a stream to form a wall-like dam. The water builds up behind into a pool. Here the beavers build a house or lodge from twigs, mud, and stones, safe from predators such as wolves, coyotes, and lynx.

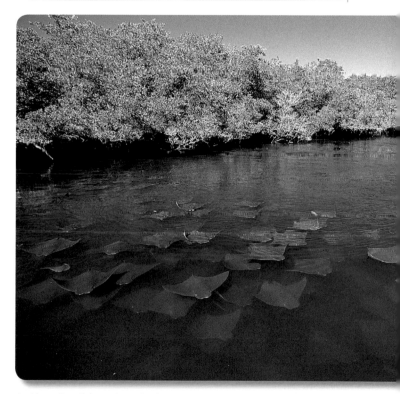

▲ Many big fish such as sharks and rays swim into coastal mangrove swamps, to lay their eggs in the sheltered waters.

DID YOU KNOW ?

The world's largest reptile lives in coastal areas such as estuaries and mangrove swamps, mainly around the Indian and west Pacific Oceans. This is the saltwater or estuarine crocodile, which grows more than 8 metres (26 feet) long.

LAKES AND PONDS

Compared to a fast river, the still water of a lake or pool does not have the problems of a fast current and few places to shelter. However, cold, moving water takes in or dissolves more oxygen from the air than the warm, still water. Tropical lakes and marshes may look ideal for wildlife, but animals and plants find survival difficult in the **stagnant**, oxygen-poor water.

▲ Rat-tailed maggots (larvae of hoverflies) survive in stagnant water by breathing air through a long tail tube.

BREATHING

Creatures have developed various adaptations to deal with the breathing problem. In the Amazon's tropical swamps some fish can gulp air into their **swim bladders** or guts. The blood-rich linings of these body parts absorb oxygen from the swallowed air, like the lungs of a land animal. One of the world's biggest freshwater fish, the arapaima (pirarucu), which grows more than 2 metres (6 feet) long, uses this method.

Lungfish have body parts that are even better adapted for breathing air, almost like real lungs. They live in South America, Africa, and Australia. Lungfish are long, slim fish resembling eels. They grow to about 1.5 metres (5 feet) long and hunt smaller fish, frogs, and other water creatures. They absorb oxygen from air when their pools become shallow and stagnant.

Hunting in the dark

Water in swamps and creeks is often muddy and cloudy, so hunting by sight is difficult. In Australia the platypus grubs in the mud for small animals using its sensitive duck-like beak. This detects tiny electrical currents given off naturally by the active muscles of its prey.

DID YOU KNOW ?

In South America the electric eel can give a shock of 500-plus volts from its muscles, to stun its victim. This fish is not a real eel but a member of the carp group.

Blood red

On a much smaller scale, worms called blood- or sludge-worms (tubifex) also survive in low-oxygen water, even polluted ponds. They live half-buried in tubes on the bottom, their bright tail ends waving in the water. The red colour is caused by extra amounts of the oxygen-carrying substance **haemoglobin** in their blood. (This is the same substance that makes our blood red.)

Adapted for lurking

Air-breathing animals of lakes and swamps do not face the problem of low oxygen levels in water. However, they still need to obtain food. The top predators are crocodiles and alligators. Their body shape is adapted to lurking almost submerged in water. The nostrils and eyes on the top of the head allow the crocodile to breathe, smell, and watch for prey. Its long jaws and many teeth grab victims in a vice-like grip. These supreme hunters have been around for more than 200 million years, since the time of the dinosaurs.

◄ The flamingo's special beak has comb-like flaps inside to strain food from water and mud.

TIDES AND WAVES

Coasts and seashores have the world's most varying conditions. Twice each day the sea level rises at high tide and floods the area with salty water. Waves crash onto the shore with massive force. As the tide falls, living things are exposed to hot Sun, drying winds, the freshwater of rain, or icy frosts. Added to all this are the usual changes of day and night and the yearly cycle of seasons. Seashore plants and animals have extremely specialized adaptations and most cannot live anywhere else.

▲ Shore-fish such as blennies and shannies have tough, rubbery, slippery skin to avoid being damaged by waves and rolling boulders.

TOUGH PLANTS

Plants along the coast are mainly types of **algae** called seaweeds. They do not have proper roots like land plants but many have root-like holdfasts that cling strongly to the rocks so they are not swept away by waves. They also have leaf-like fronds with tough, leathery, slippery surfaces that are not torn by the waves or dried out by the Sun.

RULED BY THE TIDE

Most seashore animals are not adapted to the 24-hour cycle of day and night, like animals on land. They follow the 12-hour rise and fall of the tides. Crabs, shrimps, prawns, sea-snails such as winkles and whelks, and worms such as ragworms are all active at high tide and hide away for low tide.

Some animals stay under the mud or sand. They include shellfish such as tellins, cockles, clams, and gapers. As the tide comes in they extend fleshy tubes called **siphons**. They suck in water through one siphon, filter out tiny edible particles inside their bodies, and squirt the water out of the other siphon.

▲ Sea-anemones extend their tentacles to catch prey As the tide falls they close up like blobs of jelly.

HOLDING ONTO THE ROCKS

Like seashore plants, the animals are at risk of being swept away. Crabs, fish, and other active animals find shelter in crevices or among seaweeds. Sea-snails have a broad "foot" for sticking to the rocks. The limpet has the strongest grip, and does not need to find shelter. It can clamp its low, cone-shaped shell to the rock with a force that resists the strongest waves.

▲ At low tide seaweeds such as wracks provide cool, moist shelter for seashore animals such as this crab.

TRAPPED FOR LIFE

Tides, waves, and currents continually bring seawater, containing two of life's essentials – food and oxygen. Piddocks are shellfish that burrow into solid rock by twisting and rasping their strong, spiny shells. As in other shellfish, two tubes called siphons take in water for feeding and breathing and then squirt it out. The piddock grows as it bores slowly into the rock so that it becomes too big to leave its tunnel.

DID YOU KNOW ?

The lugworm, in its U-shaped burrow, eats sand to digest any nutrient particles. It ejects the grains onto the surface above its rear end as squiggly worm casts. In one year a lugworm can eat enough sand to fill a family car!

LIFE IN THE OCEAN

The ocean is the largest habitat on Earth, bigger than all other habitats added together. Where its warm, shallow waters lap calmly towards a tropical beach, this may seem ideal for life. However, the ocean also has huge waves and strong currents. About 500 to 1,000 metres (1,650 to 3,300 feet) below the surface it is cold and dark so plants cannot grow. This presents many challenges to living things.

► Sealions in the warm, tropical waters off the coast of California

SMALL PLANTS, BIG FISH

The main plants in the ocean are microscopic **phytoplankton**. They are food for similarly small animals, **zooplankton**. Larger animals have adaptations to feed on such tiny food. The biggest fish in the world, the whale shark and basking shark, filter them from the water using frilly, comb-like parts called **rakers**. These are on the gills, the breathing parts on the side of a fish's head.

▲ Zooplankton provide a source of food for the whale shark.

LIFE AT THE SURFACE

A shark's liver is enormous and made of very oily flesh. Oil is lighter than water and the large liver helps the fish stay near the surface where plankton is most abundant. The sperm whale has the opposite problem. It is a mammal and so must surface to breathe air. Its prey of large fish and giant squid live far below in the depths. The sperm whale has great quantities of a waxy substance, called **spermaceti**, in its bulging forehead. As the whale dives this becomes more solid and denser or heavier, helping the whale to descend more than 3,000 metres (9,850 feet).

DID YOU KNOW ?

The female deep-sea anglerfish has no trouble finding a male mate in the vast, black ocean depths. He attaches onto her body and stays there, living on her like a parasite, and always ready for breeding.

ON THE DEEP OCEAN BED

More than seven-eighths of the ocean is not warm and sunlit, but cold and pitch dark. The only food is dead bodies, droppings, and other bits drifting down from above. Creatures on the bottom, such as sea-cucumbers, worms, clams, and other shellfish are mainly blind. They have no eyes because there is no light to see. Instead, their bodies are very sensitive to touch and water currents. They feed on small edible pieces in the thick mud of the seabed.

GRAB ANY PREY YOU CAN

Animals are rare in the vast, black depths of the sea. So deep-sea fish who hunt there are adapted to grab almost any prey they find. The gulper eel has a huge mouth five times bigger than its body. The viperfish has long, sharp teeth that angle backwards into its throat so that any prey it grabs cannot escape.

▲ The deep-sea gulper eel showing its huge mouth

SURVIVAL NEAR THE POLES

Some of the harshest conditions for life on Earth are found in polar lands. In the far north the ice-covered Arctic Ocean is surrounded by frozen lands, and in the south chilly seas surround the ice-covered continent of Antarctica. The main problems are intense cold and long, dark winters. Few plants can grow in such conditions, which means there is little food for animals. The cold, treeless plains of grasses, sedges, and other low plants are known as the **tundra** habitat.

◄ Reindeer walk long distances, migrating north for summer plant growth, then south for winter shelter.

SHORT SUMMERS, LONG WINTERS

The polar regions have the most extreme climate in the world. For a short time each summer the Sun never sets and the temperature rises to several degrees above freezing. Conditions are suitable for life. However, during the long winter the Sun hardly rises and the air temperature can fall below −50°C (−58°F). Within seconds any living thing would freeze solid.

SUMMER VISITORS

The winter in polar lands is too long, cold, and dark for most larger animals so they leave or migrate. In the Arctic many types of bird such as duck, geese, and plovers fly south to warmer regions for the winter. They return north in the spring to nest and raise their young.

COPING WITH WINTER

Plants and animals in polar regions have made adaptations to cope with the intense winter cold and take advantage of the brief summer growing season. The main plants are sedges and mosses. They are low-growing, out of the fierce wind. Small animals such as springtails, midges, mosquitoes, and other insects spend the winter as tough-cased eggs that hatch in spring.

WARM WHITE COATS

Warm-blooded Arctic animals include birds such as snowy owls and ptarmigan, and mammals such as polar bears, seals, voles, lemmings, snowshoe hares, and Arctic foxes. They have extra thick coats of feathers or fur and also a thick layer of fat under the skin, called **blubber**, to keep in body warmth. Most spend the long winter resting in sheltered nests in burrows, caves, or dens.

▲ Ptarmigan change their white winter plumage to brown for camouflage in the summer.

IN POLAR SEAS

The seas around Antarctica are very cold but also extremely rich in nutrients brought up from deeper waters by ocean currents. In summer they support a wide variety of life that starts with the tiny plant and animal varieties of plankton. These are eaten by small fish and shrimp-like creatures known as **krill**. In turn these are eaten by squid, larger fish, penguins, seals, and the largest animals on the planet, the great whales.

DID YOU KNOW ?

The largest animals that live permanently on the mainland of Antarctica are tiny springtails (types of insect) that are just a few millimetres long.

HEAT AND DROUGHT

Deserts may be hot or cold, sandy or rocky, windy or calm, in highlands or lowlands. The one feature they have in common is lack of water, or **drought**. Since water is vital for any form of life, deserts pose huge problems for animals and plants. However, even in these almost waterless wastes, living things have developed amazing adaptations in order to survive.

THE DESERT COMES ALIVE

The desert may look brown and lifeless for years. Then within a few days of rain, plants begin to spring up. They have been inactive or **dormant**, as seeds or as underground plant parts such as bulbs and **corms**. They are called **ephemerals** and are adapted to grow quickly while the soil is moist, producing flowers and seeds.

There are also ephemeral animals. Fairy shrimps survive drought as tough-cased eggs. These hatch quickly, grow into adults in the temporary puddles, and breed to produce the next batch of eggs. Their whole life cycle is over within a few days as the desert dries out once more.

▲ The water-holding frog of Australia survives drought underground in a watery, bag-like cocoon.

GATHERING MOISTURE

The main aim for plants and animals in the desert is to find water. Plants such as cacti spread their long, thin roots far and wide to soak up moisture from a large surface area. Cacti's leaves have become sharp spines – an adaptation to protect against plant-eating animals and moisture loss. Their stems are wide and barrel-shaped to store water. Trees such as acacias and baobabs send roots many metres down into the soil to find moisture far below.

► The darkling beetle does a headstand so that its body catches morning dew and mist, which run down into its mouth.

OUT AT NIGHT

Many desert creatures avoid the scorching daytime Sun by coming out during twilight or at night. By day smaller animals such as desert mice and kangaroo rats hide in cool burrows. Larger animals such as kangaroos and Arabian oryx rest in the shade of a tree, rock, or dune. These creatures obtain most of the moisture they need from the leaves and seeds they eat.

MOVING OVER SOFT SAND

Soft desert sand tends to shift and slip as animals move over it so various desert creatures have adapted their bodies to different ways of moving.

- Kangaroo rats, gerbils, and jerboas have large back feet and leap rather than run.
- The camel has wide feet that spread its body weight and prevent it sinking.
- Desert snakes such as the sidewinder move in a sideways fashion, almost like waves rippling on the beach. The long body pushes against the sand, giving a larger surface area so the sand grains slip less.

- Desert skinks and sandfish (types of lizard) do not walk on the surface. They wriggle through the sand itself, similar to fish swimming through water.

◄ Dromedary camels in the Sahara Desert

LIVING ON THE EDGE

A few places in the world seem so harsh and inhospitable that life could not survive. They include the ice and snow of glaciers and icebergs, hot springs where the water is almost boiling, and deep dark caves. Yet even here, living things have adapted and found a way to survive — and in some cases, to thrive. **Organisms** that adapt to these severe conditions have few predators, competitors, or rivals. This is why extreme habitats do not have many inhabitants, but those species that can survive do so in great numbers.

LIFE AFTER DEATH

After a bush fire, **pioneer** plants grow rapidly in the blackened earth. They are not adapted for a long stay. Gradually, they are crowded out by slower, steadier growers. By this time, however, they have already grown, flowered, and scattered their seeds widely.

Large trees such as black spruce, wild ginger, and labrador tree have adaptations such as thick bark that resist fire damage. Underground parts of herbs such as sage, thyme, and rosemary also survive the scorching.

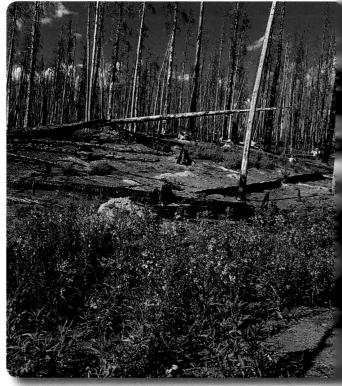

▲ Pioneer plants have sprung up here following a bush fire in Yellowstone National Park, Wyoming, USA.

DID YOU KNOW

A new island called Surtsey appeared in the North Atlantic near Iceland in 1963. At first it was bare, hot rock. By the year 2005 more than 1,000 species of plants and animals lived there.

INVADING NEW LAND

Brand new land, for example an ocean island made by a just-erupted underwater volcano, rarely stays empty. Plant seeds blow in the wind, such as the *Brachycereus* cactus that grows on new volcanic rocks. Sea creatures such as seals and turtles climb out and leave their nutrient-rich droppings. Visiting birds bring tiny eggs and small animals on their bodies, as well as plant seeds and more nutrients in their droppings. Tiny creatures such as mites and spiders also blow on the wind. Gradually, the bare land develops into a thriving habitat.

WHEN WARM

Grylloblattids are strange insects found in remote mountains such as the North American Rockies. They look like a combination of cockroach and cricket but they are a separate insect group. Grylloblattids live on glaciers and snowfields, scavenging on windblown scraps of food. Their body processes are adapted to thrive at temperatures of about 0 to 5°C (32 to 41°F). If they become much warmer they die.

▲ A grylloblattid

EXTREMES OF HEAT AND COLD

The water of some hot springs is too scalding to touch. However, **extremophile** organisms such as **bacteria** and algae grow and form crusts on the rocks. At the other end of the temperature scale are cold-loving ice-worms (*Mesenchytraeus*) that burrow through the ice of Alaska, and bacteria that live on the undersides of icebergs. These simple organisms contain unusual versions of the normal substances called **enzymes**, which break down minerals in the surroundings to get the energy for life.

▼ Hot springs support colourful heat-loving organisms.

THE URBAN JUNGLE

The fastest-spreading habitat in the world is the urban one of towns and cities. Bricks, concrete, tarmac, and mown grass may seem hostile and forbidding to wild animals and plants. Indeed most cannot survive here. However, the urban habitat has some features that are similar to certain natural surroundings. This is why certain plants and animals have adapted to town and city life. Others have done so well that we regard them as pests.

CITY CLIFFS AND CRAGS

In the wild, rock doves live and nest around cliffs and crags. The urban habitat has "cliffs" too – the walls and ledges of buildings. This similarity led rock doves to move into towns, where they feasted on leftovers and waste food. Gradually, they became urban inhabitants. Today, hundreds of major cities have large populations of their descendants, known as **feral** or town pigeons.

AT HOME IN THE TOWN

Many other animals and plants are now familiar town and city dwellers. Creatures include house mice, brown rats, grey squirrels, red foxes, gulls, starlings, spiders, ants, termites, cockroaches, and the most common of all, house flies. In many tropical regions animals such as geckos and tree frogs also frequent houses. Plants include nettles, plantains, willowherbs, and shrubs such as elder and buddleia.

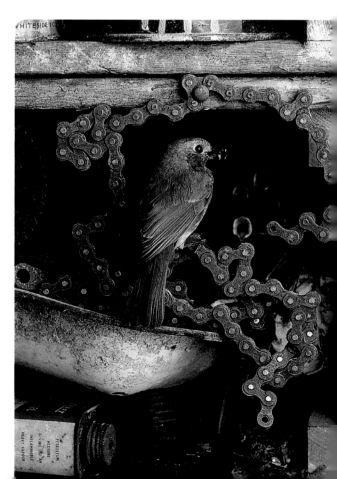

► Birds like this robin will happily nest in quiet buildings or sheds.

TAKING THE OPPORTUNITY

The wildlife that moves into towns and cities is **opportunistic**. It takes the opportunity or chance to live in the surroundings humans have created for themselves. All the essentials of life are here, such as warmth in heated buildings, and shelter in roof spaces, hollow walls, pipes, and drains. There is also plentiful food, either stored for human use or thrown away in bins and on rubbish heaps. The animals are also adaptable too. They change their behaviour and diet, eating what is available and nesting wherever they can.

UP IN THE ROOF

Barns, churches, and other big buildings are like great tree holes or caves for animals. They have been taken over by different animals in different parts of the world:

- Raccoons in North America.
- Roof rats in parts of Asia.
- Ring-tailed possums in Australia.
- Barn owls in most places, making the barn owl the world's most widespread bird.

DID YOU KNOW ?

One of the world's biggest feathered pests is the red-billed quelea. Millions of these birds devastate farm crops all across the continent of Africa.

► Many animals, especially those that scavenge in their natural habitats, for example gulls and rats, fit in well in urban habitats. The rubbish tip is like a vast supermarket for them.

GLOSSARY

adapted, adaptation feature of a living thing that helps it to fit into its surroundings, or environment, and improve its chances of survival

algae simple plants without proper flowers, stems, or roots. They include seaweeds of all kinds and also the tiny plants, phytoplankton.

anti-freeze chemical substance that does not freeze solid when it becomes very cold

bacteria minute living things, only visible under a microscope, and found almost everywhere on Earth

blubber oily or fatty layer under the skin of some animals, which helps to keep in body warmth

camouflage blending in with the surroundings, usually by shape, colour, and pattern, to be less noticeable

cold-blooded creature whose body temperature varies with the temperature of its surroundings

colony group of living things that are fairly close together in one area

corm underground part of a plant similar to a bulb. During winter the plant dies and the corm stores all the plant's nutrients until spring when the plant will grow again.

dormant sleeping; still, inactive, and not changing much

drought long time without rain or some other form of moisture, as in a desert environment

enzyme natural chemical substance inside living things that causes changes inside the body, such as breaking down or digesting food to obtain energy

ephemeral short-lived, fleeting, soon gone

epiphytic plant that grows on another one and uses it to gain height, support, and perhaps shelter

estuary river's mouth, where it opens out wide and flows into the sea

extremophile living thing that thrives in extreme or exceptional conditions such as great heat or intense cold

feral animals that were once tame or domesticated but which have escaped to become wild again

gill feathery part of an animal such as a fish, used to obtain oxygen dissolved in water

habitat distinctive type of place or surroundings, such as a woodland, mountain top, grassland, or pond

haemoglobin red substance in the blood or similar body fluid of an animal, specialized to absorb and carry oxygen around the body

hibernate when an animal becomes very inactive and goes into a deep sleep during a cold time, and its body processes slow down

krill small sea creatures similar to shrimps or prawns and in the same main animal group (crustaceans)

larva young form or stage of an animal, usually different in shape from the adult, and which spends most of its time feeding

meanders wide curves or bends in a river where it gently wanders across a flat region

migrate, migration long journey usually undertaken by animals with the changing seasons, to find improved conditions such as more food or better shelter

nocturnal active at night, during the hours of darkness

nutrient substance needed by a living thing for its growth, development, and survival

opportunistic taking any chance or opportunity that comes along

organism living thing

parasite   living thing that obtains some requirement such as food or shelter from another, called the host, and harms the host in the process

phytoplankton   tiny plants drifting in the water (see zooplankton)

pioneer   being one of the first or earliest in a new or strange place

prairie   large region of grassland where there are few trees, especially in North America

predator   living thing that hunts, catches, and kills other living things, its prey, for food

raker   comb-like part on the gills of a water animal, that filters or sieves tiny bits of food from the water

scavenge   to search for and eat dead or dying living things, remains of other predators' kills, or leftover food

siphon   in an animal, a body opening shaped like a tube that takes water in or passes it out, usually for breathing or feeding

species   a group of living things that look similar to each other and can breed together, but that cannot breed with other living things

spermaceti   waxy or oily substance inside the head of a sperm whale that helps it to dive to great depths

stagnant   still, old, or stale

symbiosis   when two different kinds (species) of living thing survive together and help or benefit each other

swim bladder   body part of a water creature such as a fish that contains bubbles of gas and helps the animal to swim, rise, and descend

temperate   average conditions, neither too hot nor too cold; usually refers to areas of the Earth which are neither very hot like the tropics or very cold like the poles

tundra   flat, treeless region in a very cold place, where the soil is frozen for part of the year

urban   to do with towns, cities, or built-up areas

warm-blooded   creature whose body temperature is controlled from within and stays fairly constant, usually above the temperature of the creature's surroundings

zooplankton   tiny animals drifting in the water (see phytoplankton)

FIND OUT MORE

Internet research

You can find out more about adaptation on the Internet. Use a search engine such as www.google.com or www.yahooligans.com to search for information. A search for "adaptation" will bring back lots of results but it may be difficult to find the information you want. Try refining your search to look for some of the specific animals, plants, or ideas mentioned in this book, such as "dippers", "cacti", or "animal camouflage".

More books to read

Hunter, Rebecca. *Science, the facts*. London: Franklin Watts, 2003

Petty, Kate. Nature files: *Animal camouflage and defence*. Oxford: Heinemann Library, 2003

Savage, Stephen. *Focus on habitats* (series). London: Wayland, 2003

INDEX